GRAMMAR
BASICS

NOUNS

KATE RIGGS

CREATIVE
PAPER BACKS

Published by Creative Paperbacks
P.O. Box 227, Mankato, Minnesota 56002
Creative Paperbacks is an imprint of The Creative Company
www.thecreativecompany.us

Design and production by Liddy Walseth
Art direction by Rita Marshall
Printed in the United States of America

Photographs by Getty Images (American Images Inc., Alistair Berg, Burazin, MoMo Productions,
Newspix, Andy Ryan, Joel Sartore, Gandee Vasan, Art Wolfe), iStockphoto (by_nicholas,
Eric Isselée, Valerii Kaliuzhnyi, Steve Snowden), Shutterstock (Jaimie Duplass)

Library of Congress Cataloging-in-Publication Data
Riggs, Kate.
Nouns / by Kate Riggs.
p. cm. — (Grammar basics)
Summary: A simple overview of nouns—the words that name things—including their uses in
sentences, their common and proper types, and how to spot singular and plural forms.
Includes bibliographical references and index.
ISBN 978-1-60818-238-1 (hardcover)
ISBN 978-0-89812-801-7 (pbk)
1. English language—Noun—Juvenile literature. I. Title.
PE1205.R57 2013
428.2—dc23   2011050689

First Edition
2 4 6 8 9 7 5 3 1

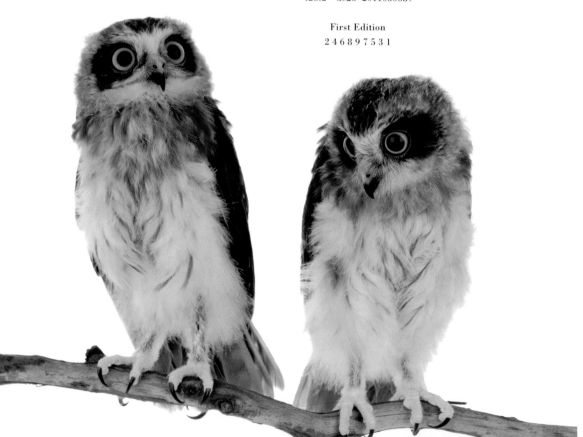

TABLE OF CONTENTS

INTRODUCTION

What do you see, hear, touch, taste, feel, or smell? You see a *house*. You hear your *friend*. You touch a *book*. You taste *ice cream*. You feel a *rock*. You smell the *grass*. All of these places, people, and things are nouns.

WHAT ARE NOUNS?

A noun is the name of something. Nouns give names to everything in the world. What is your name? You are a person. So you are a noun, too!

Three *friends* won the *race*.

NOUNS IN USE

Flamingos are colorful birds.

We use nouns when we talk. We use nouns when we write. Every **sentence** has at least one noun. The main noun in a sentence is the **subject**.

COMMON OR PROPER

Giraffes are tall *animals* from *Africa.*

There are two kinds of nouns. **Common nouns** are names for general places, people, and things. A *house*, a *dog*, and a *cookie* are common nouns. **Proper nouns** are names for certain places, people, and things. The *White House*, *Snoopy*, and *Oreos* are proper nouns.

We stacked *Oreos* on the *table.*

A CAPITAL IDEA

Did you notice something special about proper nouns? A proper noun always starts with a big letter called a capital. Use the capital clues to find the three proper nouns in this sentence:

Freddy went to Wal-Mart to buy Oreos.

WHEN ONE ISN'T ENOUGH

When we want to name more than one of something, we add –s to the noun. This is called a **plural**. Turn back to the page you just read. Do you see a plural noun? *Oreos*! This is a proper plural noun.

HUNTING FOR
PLURALS

Most of the time we use plurals with common nouns. *Houses*, *dogs*, and *cookies* are all plural common nouns. How many plural nouns can you find in the sentence below?

Mary put cakes and pies on the plates.

The four *elephants* followed the *leader*.

CHECK THE SPELLING

Sometimes a plural noun does not end in –s. It can have a different spelling. *People* means more than one person. Other times, the end of a word has to change before the –s is added.

More than one *leaf* fell from the tree. Now there are *leaves* on the ground.

Two *bees* landed on the *sunflower*.

LOOK OUT FOR NOUNS!

Nouns are the *things* we see every day. We talk to a *person* who has a name. We see *places* that have names. Every time we name something, we use a noun. So learn the names of all the nouns in your life!

Susan read a *book* in the *park.*

20

GRAMMAR GAME TIME

Have you ever played I Spy? Use the names of nouns you know to play this guessing game with a friend. Start by saying, "I spy with my little eye something that begins with A." You might see an *adult*, an *airplane*, an *animal*, or even an *ant*. Your friend will guess what the person, place, or thing is until he or she gets it right. Then it will be your friend's turn to say "I spy with my little eye. . . ." Keep playing, using a different letter of the alphabet each time, until you have named all the nouns in sight!

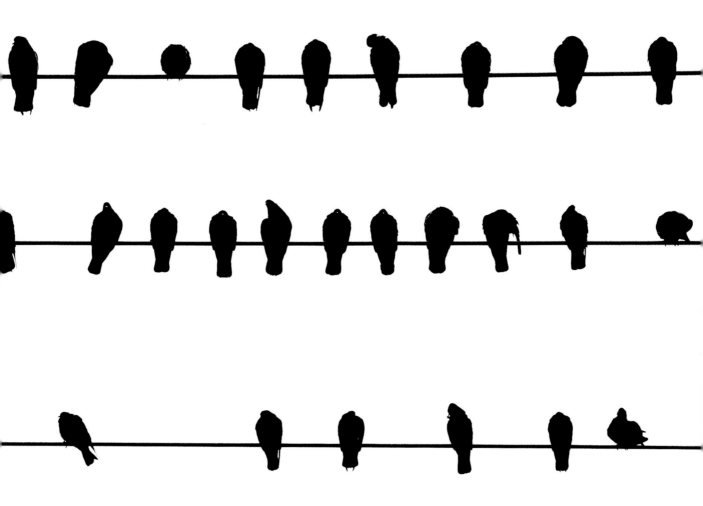

GRAMMAR WORD BANK

common nouns—non-capitalized words that name people, places, and things
plural—more than one
proper nouns—capitalized words that name certain people, places, and things
sentence—a group of words that has a noun as the subject and a verb
subject—the noun that is what or whom the sentence is about

READ MORE

Fleming, Maria. *Grammar Tales: Chicken in the City.* New York: Scholastic, 2004.

Pulver, Robin. *Nouns and Verbs Have a Field Day.* New York: Holiday House, 2006.

WEB SITES

Grammar Blast
http://www.eduplace.com/kids/hme/k_5/grammar/
Test your noun knowledge by taking the quiz at your grade level.

Grammar Gorillas
http://www.funbrain.com/grammar/index.html
Spot the noun in the sentence, and the gorilla gets a banana!

INDEX